i

SUMMARY*

Reports from most of the twelve Federal Reserve Districts indicated that economic conditions continued to expand from January to early February. Eight Districts reported improved levels of activity, but in most cases the increases were characterized as modest to moderate. New York and Philadelphia experienced a slight decline in activity, which was mostly attributed to the unusually severe weather experienced in those regions. Growth slowed in Chicago, and Kansas City reported that conditions remained stable during the reporting period. The outlook among most Districts remained optimistic.

Retail sales growth weakened since the previous report for most Districts, as severe winter weather limited activity. However, Richmond, St. Louis, and Minneapolis reported modest sales growth since the beginning of the year. Weather was also cited as a contributing factor to softer auto sales in many Districts, with the exception of Cleveland, which saw strong gains. Tourism increased in a number of Districts but declined in Philadelphia and was reported to have been mixed in New York and Minneapolis.

The demand for nonfinancial services was mixed compared with the last report; however, both Boston and San Francisco reported strong demand for technology related services. Manufacturing sales and production in several Districts were negatively impacted by severe winter weather; however, modest improvements were noted in Boston, Atlanta, Minneapolis, and Dallas.

Residential real estate markets continued to improve in several areas, albeit modestly. Boston and New York gave mixed reports on sales, and Philadelphia, Cleveland, Minneapolis, and Kansas City noted a decrease in sales. Many Districts cited low inventories of housing and continued home price appreciation. Commercial real estate leasing expanded, according to most reports, while reports on construction activity were mixed. Demand for commercial real estate

---

* Prepared at the Federal Reserve Bank of Atlanta and based on information collected before February 24, 2014. This document summarizes comments received from businesses and other contacts outside the Federal Reserve and is not a commentary on the views of Federal Reserve officials.

loans was solid in Boston, improved slightly in Dallas, and continued to grow steadily in Chicago and Kansas City.

Of the Districts that reported on agriculture, conditions softened in Kansas City and Dallas as dry soil adversely affected wheat crops. Districts reported that energy production and demand continued to increase as a result of increased demand due to the unusually cold winter.

Employment levels improved gradually for most Districts, and shortages of specialized skilled labor continued to be reported. Price pressures remained subdued, with the exception of upward cost pressures for some energy and construction products. Wage pressures remained stable for most Districts.

Consumer Spending and Tourism

Most Districts reported sales growth had softened from January to early February. New York reported noticeable weakness; however, Richmond, St. Louis, and Minneapolis reported modest growth since the beginning of the year. The extreme winter weather conditions reportedly contributed to the decline in sales in some markets; however, Richmond, Chicago, and Minneapolis reported that weather-related goods contributed to positive sales growth. Reports from furniture retailers in Boston and Minneapolis indicated strong sales. Contacts in Cleveland, Richmond, Kansas City, Dallas, and San Francisco expected retail spending to improve going forward. Vehicle sales varied across Districts. Severe weather conditions resulted in softer vehicle sales as reported by New York, Philadelphia, Richmond, Chicago, Kansas City, and Dallas. Cleveland noted a modest increase in auto sales compared with a year ago. New York cited upcoming auto shows as an expected boost for future sales, while Chicago anticipates that sales incentives will increase near-term sales.

Travel and tourism was generally strong across most reporting Districts except for Philadelphia who recorded a slight decrease. San Francisco stated that the level of travel and tourism increased in their region. Recent winter weather conditions benefited many ski resorts in Kansas City, Richmond, and Minneapolis. Atlanta and Boston also indicated that hotels fared well from the weather, but that restaurants, museums, and other attractions were negatively impacted. New York reported mixed activity from January to early February. Hotel occupancy rates in Manhattan and New Jersey increased, buoyed by the Super Bowl, while hotel business was down in western New York State due to the harsh winter storms. Airline contacts from Dallas indicated solid to slightly stronger demand, with some temporary disruptions due to severe winter weather across the nation. The majority of Districts reported a solid start in the first quarter for hotel bookings, occupancy, and revenue with an optimistic outlook for the remainder of the year.

Nonfinancial Services

Reports from Districts mentioning nonfinancial business services indicated that activity has been mixed since the previous report. Both New York and Philadelphia reported that severe winter weather reduced demand for services in their region. Activity in Minnesota and San Francisco's professional business service firms improved since their last report. Boston said that demand for software and information technology was stronger than expected, and demand for cloud computing remained strong according to San Francisco's report. Richmond service providers noted flat revenue in recent weeks, while sales were characterized as stable among Kansas City service providers. The outlook among contacts was mixed, as well. Planned activity in St. Louis was described as negative, while contacts in Minneapolis and Dallas noted optimism. Contacts in Kansas City anticipate activity will pick up, while software and IT professionals in San Francisco are cautiously optimistic and anticipate revenue growth will be positive this quarter.

Transportation activity since the previous report was mixed. Severe weather reportedly disrupted supply chains and delayed shipments in several Districts. In Dallas, railroad cargo volumes fell slightly below year earlier levels, with winter weather conditions across the country largely to blame. Port activity in Atlanta and Richmond reflected increases in auto shipments, while Dallas reported declines in container volumes. Atlanta and Dallas indicated air cargo was down, compared with year earlier levels. Kansas City cited increasing optimism about future transportation activity, while Cleveland noted expectations that demand in 2014 will be the same or only moderately higher than a year ago.

Manufacturing

Manufacturing activity expanded at a moderate pace from January through early February in most Districts. Several Districts reported that severe winter weather had a negative effect on sales and production during this period, including Boston, New York, Philadelphia, Cleveland, Richmond, Atlanta, Chicago, St. Louis, and Dallas. The weather was cited to have caused utility outages, disrupted supply chains and production schedules, and resulted in a slowing of sales to affected customers. Philadelphia and Richmond reported that shipments and orders declined during the first half of February. Steel producers in Cleveland indicated that they have excess capacity, and San Francisco reported low capacity utilization rates at steel mills. Boston and San Francisco indicated that semiconductor sales had been particularly strong. High-tech contacts in Dallas reported a slight improvement in orders, as demand for memory chips remained strong and demand for logic devices remained weak but stable. San Francisco also cited growth in the commercial aerospace industry due to a backlog in orders for commercial aircraft, while defense-related manufacturers reported sluggish overall conditions and expected sales to trend downward. Auto production was strong in Chicago despite weather-related slowdowns in sales, and Cleveland reported auto production to be higher than a year ago. Most Districts were optimistic about the future and expect manufacturing activity to rise in the coming months.

Real Estate and Construction

Reports on residential housing markets were somewhat mixed. Many Districts continued to report improving conditions but noted that growth had slowed. Most of the Districts indicating otherwise attributed the slowing pace of improvement to unusually severe winter weather conditions. Home sales increased in Richmond, Atlanta, Chicago, St. Louis, and Dallas, while sales were down in Philadelphia, Cleveland, Minneapolis, and Kansas City. Boston and New York reported that the trend in sales for their Districts was mixed. New home construction increased in Richmond, Atlanta, Chicago, St. Louis, and Minneapolis, and remained flat in Kansas City, and was down slightly from the previous period in Philadelphia. Most Districts reported low levels of home inventories and indicated that home prices continued to appreciate. The outlook for sales and residential construction was positive in Boston, Philadelphia, Cleveland, Atlanta, and San Francisco.

Strong multifamily construction was cited in New York, Cleveland, Richmond, Atlanta, and Dallas, while Boston indicated that its pipeline of multifamily construction was declining. Dallas experienced rent growth above its historical average, while New York reported mixed trends in rent growth. Cleveland noted that it expects healthy growth in rents this year.

Many Districts, including New York, Atlanta, Chicago, St. Louis, Minneapolis, Kansas City, and San Francisco, indicated that commercial real estate activity had increased and that conditions continued to improve since the previous report. Philadelphia noted that there was very little activity to report in construction or leasing due to severe winter weather. The outlook for nonresidential construction was fairly optimistic in Boston, Philadelphia, Cleveland, Atlanta, Minneapolis, Kansas City, Dallas, and San Francisco.

Banking and Financial Services

District reports of loan demand and volume were mixed. Demand for residential mortgages decreased in New York, Richmond, St. Louis, and Kansas City, and softened in Philadelphia and Dallas. Cleveland and Atlanta noted increased demand for new purchase mortgages, while mortgage refinancing declined in New York, Richmond, Atlanta, and Kansas City. Demand for consumer loans grew slightly in Philadelphia, Cleveland, Chicago, and Dallas, and held steady in Kansas City. Decreased demand for consumer loans was noted by Richmond and St. Louis, and among small to medium-sized banks in New York. Boston reported commercial real estate loans were highly competitive and demand was solid. Richmond businesses looked for shorter-term commercial real estate loans in order to benefit from lower interest rates those loans offered. Chicago and Kansas City reported steady growth in commercial real estate loans, and demand for such loans improved marginally in Dallas. Small to medium-sized banks in New York reported no change in commercial real estate loan demand.

New York noted modest declines in delinquency rates. Cleveland reported delinquencies were stable or trended lower, and St. Louis indicated delinquencies for most types of loans decreased. Loan quality in Kansas City improved compared with a year ago and continued to strengthen in Dallas. Bankers in Cleveland and Atlanta voiced concerns about recently enacted regulations and the potential negative impact on lending.

Agriculture and Natural Resources

Agricultural conditions softened since the previous report. Severe winter weather affected several Districts with some crop damage being reported by Richmond and Atlanta, while Chicago noted disruptions in the flow of agricultural products. Both Kansas City and Dallas cited dry conditions adversely affecting wheat crops, while San Francisco reported concerns about water shortages and water costs. Several Districts noted falling feed prices had a positive effect for cattle and hog producers. Kansas City indicated farmland price appreciation moderated from the rapid pace seen in the past few years. Crop prices received in January by farmers fell from a year earlier for corn, wheat, soybeans, hogs, and chickens; prices increased for cotton, rice, oranges, cattle, milk, eggs, and turkeys.

District reports showed continued strength in energy production and demand for oil and gas; much of the increased demand was driven by unusually cold winter weather. Cleveland, Richmond, and St. Louis reported coal production was down, with steam coal plant closures in Richmond. Cleveland, Atlanta, and Dallas described growth in drilling (both inland and offshore) and refining activity. In contrast, Minneapolis indicated that oil and gas exploration decreased slightly from recent months, primarily due to the extremely cold weather. Inventory drawdowns and supply shortages of natural gas and propane were reported in Atlanta, Chicago, and Dallas due to increased withdrawals that were exacerbated by the severe weather. Nearly all Districts attributed energy price surges to increased demand during the unusually cold weather; yet, Boston reported that natural gas prices were also driven up by pressure on pipeline capacity in New England. Some firms in the Richmond and Chicago Districts indicated that they elected to delay production and/or reduce usage rather than pay high prices. Dallas indicated that increases in the price of West Texas Intermediate (WTI) crude oil were being bolstered by debottlenecking at Cushing, Oklahoma.

Employment, Wages, and Prices

Since the previous report, the pace of hiring had reportedly softened in Boston, Richmond, and Chicago, with those Districts attributing at least part of the recent slowdown to unusually bad winter weather. Despite a pickup in hiring in some sectors across New York, Cleveland, Atlanta, and St. Louis, notably in manufacturing, overall employment growth for these Districts remained sluggish. In Philadelphia, as outlooks for long-term overall economic growth improved, firms reportedly continued to expand their headcounts cautiously. In contrast, labor markets in the Minneapolis District tightened slightly. The rate at which temporary employees were converted to permanent hires remained strong across Boston, while contacts in Richmond reported this conversion was happening at a slightly faster pace than previously noted. Many Districts continued to note shortages for particular types of specialized, technical skilled labor, such as healthcare professionals and information technology workers. Atlanta and Dallas also noted shortages for freight truck drivers.

Inflation pressures remained largely unchanged across most Districts. Price pressures were described as minimal or roughly steady in Boston, New York, Philadelphia, Cleveland, Atlanta, Chicago, Minneapolis, Dallas, and San Francisco. There were some mentions of rising raw materials prices passing through to final goods. Boston indicated that higher material costs and rising costs of overseas labor could have an upward influence on apparel prices. Chicago, Minneapolis, and Dallas noted that unseasonably cold weather had pushed up costs for some energy products. Construction materials prices remained a source of upward cost pressure, according to contacts in Atlanta and Kansas City. Retail contacts in New York and Philadelphia reported deep product discounting; however, reports from Dallas indicated that retail prices were stable.

Most Districts noted that wage pressures were largely steady since the last report; however, a few Districts cited upward wage pressures in some highly skilled jobs in industries such as information technology, transportation, and construction. Reports from Cleveland, Kansas City, and San Francisco indicated that businesses were anticipating wage growth to increase from the recent mild pace as the year progresses. Contacts in Chicago indicated that higher healthcare premiums increased non-wage labor costs, while a growing number of employers in Cleveland reported passing through rising healthcare costs to their employees.

FIRST DISTRICT – BOSTON

Business contacts in the First District continue to report modest increases in revenues and sales. Respondents in several sectors cite negative effects of severe winter weather. Firms report little hiring and wage increases remain very modest. Price pressures are reportedly minimal, but a few contacts note specific items for which prices are rising or are expected to rise. The outlook is generally positive, albeit cautiously so.

Retail and Tourism

This round's retail contacts completed their 2013 fiscal years at the end of December or in mid-February. Most report 2013 year-over-year sales increases ranging from 3 percent to the mid-single digits, though one cites an increase in the mid-teens. Several respondents report continued good results so far in 2014, but two retailers indicate that the pace of sales has slowed a bit. Some of this softness is said to be due to weather-related issues or to tough year-over-year comparisons with the post-Hurricane Sandy rebound. A furniture retailer reports that President's Day sales were extremely strong. Prices remain steady overall, though contacts say a modest increase in apparel prices is coming, reflecting a rise in some raw material prices and overseas labor costs. Retail respondents expect continued overall improvement in U.S. economic conditions and consumer sentiment in 2014.

Boston area hotels attained new record highs for hotel occupancy rates and revenues in 2013, building on the strong records sent in 2012. Expectations are for continued strong growth in 2014, though hotels expect to see revenue growth but not increases in occupancy rates; these are forecast at 80 percent, a 1 percentage point increase over 2013. Severe winter weather in January and February had hotels faring well, but restaurants, museums, and other venues losing revenue due to the harsh weather conditions. An industry contact says that this pattern seems to hold for much of the eastern seaboard.

Manufacturing and Related Services

Of 13 manufacturers contacted this round, nine report higher sales than the same period a year earlier. Two firms, a toy manufacturer and a publisher, cite flat sales but the reasons appear to be idiosyncratic. Two others, a manufacturer of electrical equipment for residential and commercial buildings and a maker of membranes, report falling sales but both attribute the drop to the weather. The direct effect of the storms was the loss of several days of production in February. In addition, demand fell both because some of their products are intermediate goods for other plants in afflicted areas and because end users demanded less. For example, reduced construction meant that there was less demand for electrical supplies. Three firms in the semiconductor industry report strong sales, confirming the end of that sector's slowdown, which began in 2011. Two firms, a maker of electrical equipment and a tool maker, both reported that residential investment was a significant driver of growth.

The news on inventories is mixed. Six contacts say that they continue to make a concerted effort to reduce inventories. However, one contact was building inventory on the assumption that the drop in sales due to the winter weather would lead to an increase in demand in the second quarter to make up for it. An electrical equipment supplier said that in some product lines, bad weather led to higher demand for replacement parts which reduced inventories. None of our contacts report any major pricing pressure, up or down, either from suppliers or customers. One contact said that pressure on pipeline capacity in New England is driving up natural gas prices.

Most firms report increased capital spending in 2013 and plans to increase again in 2014. However, most of those plans were already in place and there is little evidence of positive revisions in recent months. Five contacts report flat employment, four note positive hiring, and four cite reduced staffing. Respondents say engineering staff remains somewhat difficult to find, but otherwise none of our contacts have complaints about the labor market.

Eleven of 13 contacts report positive or very positive outlooks for 2014. The exceptions are a toy maker, who is generally cautious, and a publisher anticipating falling sales.

Software and Information Technology Services

First District software and information technology services contacts generally report stronger-than-expected business activity through February, with revenue growth exceeding earlier forecasts. For example, a healthcare contact expected a large year-over-year revenue decline due to the expiration of federal stimulus for health records software; however, the firm ended the year with just a marginal dip in revenues and positive net income growth. Only one contact, a provider of payment and banking software, reports accelerated growth, with year-over-year revenue increases in the 15 percent range. The majority of firms are maintaining headcount; one contact added positions in sales and marketing. Wages remain steady, with firms awarding (and in one case reinstating) merit increases in the 2.5 percent to 3.5 percent range. Both selling prices and capital and technology spending have gone largely unchanged. The outlook among software and IT contacts is cautious optimism, with expectations of modest revenue growth through the end of the quarter. Contacts remain concerned about general macroeconomic conditions and uncertainty surrounding healthcare reform.

Staffing Services

New England staffing contacts report softened business conditions in recent months, attributed to both the holiday season and the large number of snowstorms occurring throughout the Northeast. Although revenues are up slightly year-over-year, they are down on a quarter-over-quarter basis. Despite these difficulties, labor demand remains strong across most industries, with contacts noting particularly high demand in the software, engineering, legal, specialty manufacturing, and healthcare sectors. Demand has weakened in the defense sector. On the supply side, contacts cite a shortage of candidates to fill nursing, specialized manufacturing, and IT roles. This reportedly reflects a skills mismatch, amplified by the holidays and severe weather. In response, firms continue to invest in social media initiatives to reach a broader audience of candidates. The temporary-to-permanent conversion rate remains strong. Bill rates and pay rates have generally held steady, with the exception of two contacts reporting an upward trend in pay rates and one contact reporting a slight increase in bill rates. Looking forward, staffing contacts are optimistic that growth will accelerate as weather conditions improve, expecting mid-single-digit revenue growth through the next few months. Several contacts express concerns about continued uncertainty regarding how healthcare reform will affect the staffing industry.

Commercial Real Estate

Commercial real estate activity was mixed across the First District, but contacts report that leasing fundamentals were largely stable in recent weeks. In Providence, demand for multifamily housing remains strong downtown, while industrial leasing activity is still weak. In Boston, office demand continues to be uneven within the city, with strength in the Seaport District, increasing demand in some suburban areas, and comparative weakness—including downward pressure on rents—in the Financial District. In Boston and Hartford, severe winter weather modestly reduced office leasing inquiries. Also, according to one contact, investment sales activity slowed in the region in the aftermath of a year-end surge in transactions. At the same time, contacts indicate that investment demand for commercial real estate remains strong across the region, and especially strong in Boston. A Portland contact characterizes leasing activity as solid and notes that land sales continue to gather momentum. Planned developments in Portland include a diverse mix of structures: recreational facilities, hotels, office space, and specialty retail. According to a regional banking contact, the bank lending environment for commercial real estate remains highly competitive, with solid loan demand across numerous sectors, albeit including fewer condominium development loans than had been expected. Recent trends in construction activity persist, with slow growth in the institutional sector, a declining pipeline of multifamily structures, and an increase in planned mixed-use developments and speculative office construction in parts of Boston.

While contacts are mostly optimistic concerning the outlook for commercial real estate in their respective markets, some downside risks are noted, including renewed macroeconomic uncertainty stemming from recent, weaker-than-expected employment reports, an uncertain future path of interest rates, and fallout from unrest in the Ukraine, Syria, and Venezuela. Other factors seen as restraining growth include rising construction and maintenance costs, and, in Rhode Island, political stagnation stemming from the current gubernatorial election.

Residential Real Estate

The First District experienced mixed results for sales of single family houses and condominiums in December. Contacts in New Hampshire and Rhode Island cite declines in sales of single family homes, while Massachusetts experienced no change, and respondents in Connecticut, Maine, and Vermont cite increases in sales relative to December 2012. Scarce inventory is said to be the most significant constraint on the growth of sales, while uncertainty from new qualified mortgage rules and flood insurance reforms are also believed to be causing buyers to remain cautious about making offers. Contacts in Connecticut say that sales are being affected by weak consumer confidence and a shortage of stable employment opportunities. Median sale prices increased year-over-year in four of the six New England states, decreasing only in Connecticut and Vermont. In Massachusetts, particularly in the Greater Boston area, price appreciation driven by low inventory levels has become a concern as realtors caution that high prices could keep first time home buyers out of the market.

Pending sales suggest the market for single family houses and condos is off to a good start in 2014, increasing in all states except Rhode Island. Contacts express optimism about local housing markets looking forward but say they expect the snowy winter to depress sales in the near term.

SECOND DISTRICT--NEW YORK

Economic activity in the Second District declined modestly in the first few weeks of 2014, hampered by inclement weather. Contacts report some broadening of price pressures in the service sector, though retail prices remain mostly stable. Manufacturers in the District report that activity was stable whereas service-sector firms report some weakening, on balance. 'Labor market conditions have continued to improve gradually since the last report. General merchandise retailers report that sales were below plan and down sharply from a year earlier, due to unusually harsh weather in January and early February. New auto sales weakened noticeably in January but showed signs of rebounding in the first half of February. Tourism activity was mixed in January and early February, hampered by harsh weather but boosted by the Super Bowl. Housing markets were mixed, while commercial real estate markets firmed slightly. Finally, banks report some further weakening in loan demand from the household sector, little change in credit standards, and steady to declining delinquency rates.

Consumer Spending

General merchandise retailers report that sales weakened noticeably in early 2014, running below plan and well below year-ago levels. Two major retail chains indicate that sales during the first six weeks of the year were down sharply from comparable 2013 levels, mainly due to the weather. One contact notes exceptionally low gift card redemptions—viewed as a likely harbinger that much of the shortfall in sales will be made up when warmer weather arrives. Similarly, contacts at major malls in upstate New York report that sales were weak in January and early February, due largely to heavy snow and extremely cold weather, particularly during weekends. Not surprisingly, one category that has performed reasonably well is cold-weather outerwear. Inventories are mostly at or modestly above desired levels. Prices are reported to be little changed, though some retail contacts describe the environment as increasingly promotional.

After a strong 2013, auto dealers in upstate New York report that new vehicle sales weakened noticeably in January but showed some signs of rebounding in early February. Inclement weather is viewed as having been an inhibiting factor in January, but not the only one; conversely, some of the pickup in February is attributed to a major auto show in Buffalo, and an upcoming show in Rochester is expected to provide some boost as well. Wholesale and retail credit conditions for auto purchases remain favorable.

Tourism activity has been mixed thus far in 2014. Despite the bad weather, attendance at Broadway theaters is up about 7 percent year-to-date, form 2013 levels, and total revenues are up 12 percent; however, it should be noted that there are roughly 15 percent more shows running in 2014 than in 2013. Manhattan hotels report that occupancy rates were little changed from a year earlier in January, though room rates were up sharply—cold and snowy weather dampened demand but this was largely offset by business related to the Super Bowl, which buoyed occupancy and especially room rates in late January and early February. Hotels in northern New Jersey, where occupancy rates are typically much lower this time of year, reportedly saw a more pronounced boost during the weeks around the Super Bowl. Hotels in western New York State, on the other hand, report that winter storms depressed business in January—particularly in Rochester and Niagara Falls.

Finally, consumer confidence improved in January: the Conference Board's surveys of residents of both the Middle Atlantic states (NY, NJ, Pa) and New York alone show confidence surging to a six-year high, while Siena College's survey of New York State residents indicates a more moderate increase, to a six-month high.

Construction and Real Estate

The District's housing markets have been mixed since the last report. Contacts in western New York State note some softening in both activity and prices in early 2014—largely a function of the unusually cold and snowy weather, but also reflecting increased difficulty obtaining credit. More broadly, though, home sales across New York State showed resilience in January, slipping only slightly from the elevated level of a year earlier, while prices reportedly rose 10 percent. Sales activity in New York City's co-op and condo market slowed somewhat in January and early February, as weather greatly inhibited buyer traffic. Sales prices for apartments were flat in Manhattan but continued to trend up in Brooklyn. Similarly, the market for apartment rentals has remained steady, with rents edging down in Manhattan but rising in Brooklyn. Weather has also been a factor in northern New Jersey since mid-December for both sales and new construction, though the underlying fundamentals also remain weak: mortgage delinquencies remain high, and a stubbornly high inventory of distressed properties is dampening market conditions. The multi-family market in northern New Jersey (mostly rentals) is reported to be faring well.

Commercial real estate markets were stable to slightly stronger in early 2014. In New York City, office leasing activity was characterized as very brisk; but this was accompanied by several new spaces becoming available in both Downtown and Midtown Manhattan, leaving the overall availability rate little changed. Asking rents for office space, however, continued to rise and were up 6 to 9 percent from a year earlier. Elsewhere around the District both office availability rates and rents were little changed in early 2014. In general, the market for prime (Class A) space has underperformed the rest of the office market. Industrial vacancy rates were mostly steady to down slightly across the District, while asking rents were little changed.

Other Business Activity

The labor market has shown further signs of gradual improvement in early 2014. Business contacts in both the manufacturing and service sector report steady to rising employment; and more firms plan to increase than reduce staffing levels in the months ahead—particularly in the manufacturing sector. Separately, a major employment agency specializing in office jobs reports that the market continues to improve gradually, though weather appears to have been somewhat of a deterrent to hiring. Many job postings are challenging to fill because they call for specialized skills; salaries generally remain flat.

Manufacturing firms in the District report a slight pickup in activity in early 2014, on net, whereas service sector businesses have seen a pullback—apparently driven, in large part, by the inclement weather. Still, business contacts remain widely optimistic about the near-term outlook. Overall, price pressures remain stable and generally subdued in the manufacturing sector but have grown increasingly widespread among service-sector businesses.

Financial Developments

Small to medium-sized banks across the District report a further decrease in demand for consumer loans and residential mortgages but no change in demand for commercial mortgages and commercial & industrial loans. Bankers also indicate a decrease in demand for refinancing. Respondents note that credit standards were unchanged across all loan categories. Respondents indicate a decrease in spreads of loan rates over costs of funds for commercial loans and commercial & industrial loans, but report no change in other categories. Respondents indicate little or no change in average deposit rates. Finally, bankers report modest declines in delinquency rates, on balance, for all loan categories.

THIRD DISTRICT – PHILADELPHIA

Severe winter weather caused aggregate business activity in the Third District to decline slightly during the current Beige Book period (beginning with the first full week of January). Nearly all sectors were impacted; however, only a few sectors are expected to suffer permanent losses, according to contacts. For example, while many general retailers have had to realize their losses by heavily discounting their winter inventory, auto dealers anticipate a release of pent-up demand when spring arrives.

The general services sector was the only one to maintain some growth in this period, but even it slowed to a modest growth rate. After growing in the previous Beige Book period, general retail sales and residential construction declined moderately; auto sales, existing home sales, and commercial real estate construction declined modestly; and manufacturing, commercial leasing activity, and tourism declined slightly. Staffing services showed little net change after growing modestly over previous periods. Lending volumes also changed little change this period but credit quality continued to improve. Contacts reported slight overall increases in wages, home prices, and general price levels – similar to the last Beige Book period.

Despite the temporary declines in many sectors, most contacts remained optimistic although they now expect only modest growth over the next six months. Contacts in most sectors continued to express confidence in the underlying economy. In regard to hiring and capital expenditure plans, firms continued to expand cautiously.

Manufacturing. Third District manufacturers reported deteriorating levels of activity through the current Beige Book period, as severe winter weather repeatedly disrupted sales and production. A slight pace of growth in orders and shipments as reported for the last period continued for several weeks then gave way to slight overall declines by the end of this Beige Book period. The share of all firms reporting increases in general activity fell from about one-third to one-fourth, while the share reporting decreases rose from about one-fourth to one-third. The makers of paper products, fabricated metals, industrial machinery, and instruments have reported gains since the last Beige Book. Reports of decreases came from the makers of food products, chemicals, primary metals, and electronic and other electric equipment. About 40 percent of manufacturers cited negative impacts from the severe winter weather, including lower demand or sales, disruptions to supply channels and to deliveries, fuel and power outages, lost production days, and cost of snow removal.

Optimism that business conditions will improve over the next six months remained nearly as high as last period and continued to be widespread across sectors. Over half of the firms continued to anticipate increases in activity; however, firms were somewhat less optimistic about new orders and shipments six months out. Contacts reported similar expectations of future hiring and greater expenditures for future capital spending plans than during the prior Beige Book.

Retail. Third District retailers reported that malls and stores lost shopping days to snow storms and power outages, including significant holiday weekends, resulting in an overall moderate decline in sales since the last Beige Book. According to one mall contact, Valentine's Day weekend typically accounts for 40 percent of February sales, but the holiday's sales were off 40 percent this year due to a weekend snowstorm. Retailers have engaged in heavy discounting to move winter gear due to a dearth of shoppers. Also, spring inventory is not moving yet. In addition, retailers' margins have eroded from higher heating bills and snow removal costs. Brick-and-mortar retailers expressed uncertainty as to whether consumers have held on to their holiday gift cards or used them at online retailers. Although most of the lost sales opportunities are gone, retailers are hopeful that some pent-up demand will emerge as temperatures rise and that the prior pace of retail sales growth will resume.

Auto dealers have reported a modest decline in sales since the last Beige Book period – another casualty of the recurring winter snowstorms. Dealers' lots were covered with snow; car buyers were scarce. Pennsylvania dealers expect sales to be off at least 15 percent (year over year) in February, while January sales were up a little. New Jersey dealers reported relative softness, adjusting for seasonal trends through January, although last year's comparative sales were boosted by replacement vehicles following Hurricane Sandy. Contacts in both states described dealers as currently "pretty grouchy, but upbeat for the year." Auto dealers harbor greater hopes than general retailers that spring sales will capture pent-up demand from the winter losses. The outlook for 2014 remains positive.

Finance. Third District financial firms reported little overall change in total loan volume. Many loan categories appeared to decline slightly in volume. Credit card lending fell faster; however, that is a typical seasonal trend as consumers pay down their post-holiday balances. In contrast, other consumer credit loans and home equity lines have grown slightly since the last Beige Book period. Contacts continued to characterize the lending environment as steady, very slow, and highly competitive. Real estate lending softened considerably as the wintry weather reduced the pace of new contracts. Despite this current softness, contacts described an improving lending environment with a stronger labor market, greater consumer confidence, and healthier balance sheets. Overall, most bankers remained optimistic for continued slow, steady growth and for some pickup from pent-up demand for housing, autos, and other loans when the spring thaw finally arrives.

Real Estate and Construction. Third District homebuilders have reported that both new home sales and construction activity were depressed by the unusually severe winter weather, generating moderate declines from the prior-period construction levels. One builder reported production at 60 percent of plan, while sales were only about 50 percent of plan. Builders expect to accelerate production and catch up with prior schedules as the weather permits, and they are hopeful that spring sales may rebound. However, extra overtime coupled with increased demand from future sales may create labor shortages and escalate other input costs. According to residential real estate brokers, sales of existing homes were flat to down (year over year) in many of the Third District's major metropolitan areas in January. Pending sales and new listings were also reported as declining at a modest pace; February closings, traffic, and sales are expected to be negative throughout most of the District. Brokers are somewhat less bullish for a significant increase in 2014 over 2013 levels.

Nonresidential real estate contacts indicated some weather disruptions have delayed ongoing construction activity. Modest declines in current construction are expected to be offset in the near future as contractors hustle to resume their schedules. Leasing activity was quiet – as businesses were often shuttered – but is expected to resume its modest pace next period. Little change was reported in leasing activity. Two more major buildings were announced for Center City Philadelphia since the last Beige Book: a 59-story major office tower and a 32-story residential tower. Added to the two 47-story office/residential towers already slated for groundbreaking in 2014, these four projects have caused most contacts to become increasingly optimistic for stronger growth as the year progresses. Meanwhile, most contacts speak of incremental improvement, despite the winter lull.

Services. Third District service-sector firms have slowed to a modest pace of growth since the last Beige Book – again with weather dampening demand for a variety of services. Although the District's ski resorts benefited from the additional snowfall, even they were plagued by the storms' timing, which made travel to the resorts difficult on several weekends. In addition, school districts that have amassed too many snow days may shorten spring breaks resulting in cancelation of vacation bookings. Some have already interfered with the Presidents' Day weekend by holding classes.

Other service firms reported mostly modest growth rates – whittled down from recent moderate rates, as heavy snowfalls and power outages prevented workers from commuting and businesses from opening. As with general retail, some of the service-sector revenue will not be recouped after the snow has melted. For example, staffing firms cite the loss of billable hours that will not be made up. Other segments of the staffing industry offset those losses with slight growth. Overall, most of service-sector losses were viewed as manageable, and most contacts expect current activity to resume and grow.

Prices and Wages. Overall, Third District contacts reported no change to the steady, slight pace of price level increases, similar to other recent Beige Books. Manufacturing firms reported that prices paid and prices received tended to rise slightly, but more modestly than before. Auto dealers reported little change in pricing, general retailers reported deep discounting, and most builders reported holding prices steady. Many contacts continued to report tight, or narrowing, margins. Generally, real estate contacts continued to report rising prices for lower-priced homes, while higher-priced homes are aligned to local market conditions. Very few contacts are seeing wage pressures, other than for a few highly skilled occupations.

FOURTH DISTRICT – CLEVELAND

Overall business activity in the Fourth District continued at a moderate pace early in 2014. While the severe weather contributed to some temporary slowing across industry sectors, it was viewed mainly as an inconvenience. Demand for manufactured products remained at a moderate to robust level. Activity in the construction sector slackened a bit compared to the same time period a year ago. Post-holiday retail purchases were characterized as disappointing. In contrast, January's auto sales showed strong gains month-over-month. The energy sector was little changed: shale gas activity stayed at a high level, and coal production trended lower. Freight volume was slightly higher. Demand for business credit showed little movement, whereas consumer credit usage was somewhat better than expected.

Hiring was sluggish across most industry sectors, though we are seeing a pickup in manufacturing jobs. Staffing-firm representatives reported that the number of job openings is trending higher, while placements are flat. Vacancies were found primarily in manufacturing and healthcare. Wage pressures were contained. Input and finished goods prices saw little change, apart from some increases in building materials, energy, and diesel fuel.

Manufacturing. Reports from District factories indicated that demand stayed at a moderate to robust level during the past six weeks. Any production declines were attributed to the severe winter weather disrupting raw material deliveries or to seasonal variation. Supply chain disruptions were viewed more as an annoyance than an event that could negatively impact business activity. Compared to a year ago, production levels were generally consistent or somewhat higher. Almost all of our respondents expect production will rise relative to current levels in the upcoming months, with the strongest demand coming from the aerospace, capital equipment, housing, and oil and gas industries. Since the beginning of the year, steel shipments grew slightly—mainly a seasonal effect. Producers predicted that their industry will not exhibit strong growth until there is considerable strengthening in the construction sector and a greater sense of confidence in the economy at large. Steel shipments for the remainder of the first quarter are expected to pick up only slightly. Auto production at District plants increased along seasonal trends during January on a month-over-month basis. Compared to a year ago, production was moderately higher.

Several factory representatives commented that capacity utilization rates were above their normal range or were increasing in the last six weeks, while steel producers noted significant open capacity. Capital budgets for 2014 are generally higher than last year, although very few contacts are allocating monies for capacity expansion. Outlays are being used primarily for equipment purchases, product development, and maintenance. Raw material prices were mainly flat to lower. We heard a few reports of an upward drift in scrap metal and agricultural commodity prices after coming off of last year's low level. Energy prices (electricity and natural gas) rose, which was attributed to the severe weather. Some producers of industrial durables raised prices at the beginning of the year with little pushback. Otherwise, most manufacturers reported that their ability to raise prices has been limited. Job markets are showing some signs of strengthening, with half of our respondents indicating that they are hiring production and salaried workers. Wage increases are expected to be slightly higher in 2014 compared to the past couple of years. A growing number of employers are passing through rising healthcare costs to their employees.

Construction. Sales of new and existing single-family homes across much of the District were significantly higher in 2013 relative to the prior year, while average sale prices showed a moderate increase. Builders reported that sales of new single-family homes slowed during the first few weeks of 2014, which they attributed to the extreme cold. Web traffic trended higher. New-home contracts were found mainly in the mid-price category, and the selling prices of new homes continued to stabilize. Reports indicated that multifamily housing remains the strongest segment in the District's construction sector, and some believe there is a risk of overbuilding. Nonetheless, rents are expected to rise 3 to 4 percent this year. Builders anticipate that the housing market will grow at a steady pace in 2014.

The pace of activity in nonresidential construction has slowed a bit relative to the same time period a year ago. Builders said that while inquiries, many from first-time customers, are strong, projects keep dropping out of the pipeline due to financing issues or a last minute decision not to proceed. Backlogs are down slightly, and the severe winter weather has slowed fieldwork. Demand was strongest for industrial and institutional building, including flex-space, distribution, manufacturing, student housing, and senior living. Our contacts remain fairly optimistic about near-term prospects, and they are anticipating moderate growth this year.

Prices for drywall, steel, and plumbing fixtures are trending higher. General contractors reported satisfaction with current staffing levels and will only hire for replacement or if business activity rises above expectations. Reports of rising costs related to healthcare were widespread. There is concern among small builders that employees may lose their employer-paid insurance. One report indicated that a growing number of builders are offering employees a lump sum payment to purchase their own health insurance rather than offering it as a benefit.

Consumer Spending. Almost all retailers we contacted expressed disappointment with January sales. Revenues were below those seen in December, and they were down compared to a year earlier. Cold-weather gear and consumables were in highest demand. Most of the decline was attributed to persistently poor weather conditions. However, two retailers commented that part of the decline is related to a fundamental shift in how consumers spend money. A furniture dealer reported that his customers are less inclined to buy quality goods that can be handed down. Rather, consumers are buying only what they need and are looking for the best value. Projections for the second quarter call for sales to be modestly higher relative to those in the first quarter. Vendor and shelf prices held steady, though a few retailers noted that they are running more promotions than normal. One contact reported that he has been introducing more products at a lower price point. This year's capital budgets will be mainly higher than in 2013. Most of the monies are allocated for opening new stores and e-commerce expansion. Hiring will be limited to staffing new stores and e-commerce support.

The number of new motor vehicles sold in January was significantly higher than in December. On a year-over-year basis, sales showed a modest increase. Buyers continued to shift from smaller, fuel-efficient cars to SUVs, crossovers, and light trucks. One dealer told us that truck sales in the southwest region of the District rose 11 percent last year, which he believes reflects an uptick in commercial and construction activity. New-vehicle inventories were described as slightly elevated, which was attributed to leftover 2013 models and the extreme weather. Used-vehicle purchases during January were slightly ahead of those in December and on a year-over-year basis. Expectations for sales of new and used vehicles are positive. Dealers cited the arrival of income tax returns and interest generated by regional auto shows. Used inventory will start building due to the expiration of 2011 leases. Payrolls held steady.

Banking. Demand for business credit showed little movement. Brisk competition continues to put downward pressure on loan pricing. Consumer credit demand grew slightly since our last report, primarily for auto loans and home equity products. Residential mortgage activity picked up a little, more so in the new-purchase market. Several bankers raised concerns about recently enacted regulations and their potential negative impact on lending. Delinquency rates were stable or trended lower. Bankers reported no significant changes to loan-application standards. On net, core deposits were flat: increases by consumers were offset by declines in commercial deposits. Little net growth in staffing is expected. Many new job openings are in the areas of regulatory compliance and IT.

Energy. January's aggregate coal production across the District fell below year-ago levels. Going forward, little change in output is projected. Spot prices for metallurgical and steam coal were flat. The number of drilling rigs in Ohio's Utica shale region has increased since the beginning of the year. Natural gas production was stable and continuing at a high level. Cold weather helped boost wellhead prices for natural gas and oil. Reports on capital spending were mixed, although one respondent commented that his firm plans to increase funding to its drilling-program in Marcellus and Utica shales by 80 percent year-over-year. Production equipment and materials prices were flat. Hiring was for replacement only.

Freight Transportation. Freight executives reported that it is difficult to gauge changes in shipping volume due to supply chain disruptions attributed to severe weather. Nonetheless, most respondents believe volume has risen slightly year-over-year. Shipments of motor vehicles and machinery were strong. The industry outlook for 2014 is somewhat less favorable than in our previous report. Most of our contacts now expect volume will be in-line or moderately higher than a year ago. Recently enacted environmental and safety regulations are constraining capacity and putting upward pressure on rates. Diesel fuel prices moved higher in January. Operators have been unable to pass through the entire increase via surcharges. Reports on capital spending plans for 2014 were mixed. The industry is hiring primarily for replacement and to maintain capacity.

FIFTH DISTRICT–RICHMOND

Overview. Economic activity in the Fifth District increased modestly on balance, despite snow, ice, and unusually cold temperatures that caused many business closings. Manufacturing operations generally slowed as winter storms closed some plants, although a few firms reported an uptick in new orders. Retail sales increased modestly overall, even though many stores and auto dealerships closed during the snow storms. While some retailers benefitted from increased demand for cold-weather items, auto sales declined. Non-retail service providers reported flat revenues in recent weeks. In contrast, tourism and corporate travel picked up, and hoteliers reported strong bookings. Consumer borrowing slowed since the start of the year, while commercial lending remained strong, with several bankers reporting a healthy pipeline for business lending. Residential real estate strengthened, with Realtors reporting faster absorption in some submarkets. In addition, construction of single family homes has been slowly improving, while multi-family housing remained strong. Non-residential construction was generally soft. Commercial leasing ranged from no change to a slight increase since our last report. Agricultural activity slowed seasonally, while contacts were optimistic about a good year ahead. In the energy sector, natural gas production accelerated. In contrast, coal mining fell and some steam coal plants closed. District labor markets were mixed in recent weeks, as extreme weather affected production and services. However, demand was high for semi-skilled workers; also, more quality temp employees were being offered permanent work. According to our latest survey, employment declined at retail establishments and increased at non-retail services firms, while average wages rose across the service sector. Manufacturing employment slowed and average wages ticked up. Service sector prices advanced more quickly, while manufacturing prices increased at a slower pace.

Manufacturing. Manufacturing activity slowed in recent weeks, with winter storms affecting business operations throughout the District. There were a few weather-related plant closures since our last report, totaling between three and four days. In one instance, a North Carolina food manufacturer stated that recent storms caused his plant to close for a few days, resulting in lost wages, hours, and production. A few District plant managers said that the facility downtime would reduce shipments, and in February, survey respondents also indicated that shipments and new orders declined. However, some manufacturers reported that new orders have risen slightly and plants are working to catch up after a slow start in January. A metals manufacturer in South Carolina reported an increase in January sales, slight growth in export sales, and a stronger March forecast. Overall, contacts expected improvement in the spring. Prices of raw materials and finished goods rose at a slower pace, according to our survey.

Ports. Reports from port officials were mixed but indicated that activity increased overall. Auto imports remained robust, and container volume continued to be strong and growing year over year, particularly at the Port of Virginia. Exports of agricultural materials leveled off in Baltimore, while in

Charleston, South Carolina, exports of containerized grains and soybeans were very strong. International coal exports declined slightly while coal shipments to domestic locations fell sharply. Dockworkers at the Port of Baltimore with unresolved labor contracts have remained on the job as mediators work toward a conclusion. Seasonal slowdowns related to the Chinese New Year are expected to last into mid-March.

Retail. District retailers reported modest revenue growth, restrained in part by the unusually cold temperatures and multiple winter storms that forced many stores and auto dealerships to close temporarily. An auto dealership in West Virginia reported getting 18 to 20 inches of snow, with only one customer on the lot the next day. Sales of weather-related goods were up for a chain hardware merchant in central Virginia, and the manager of a West Virginia sporting goods store said that the weather helped sales, despite declining foot traffic. Post-holiday discounting boosted sales at several stores in January following mediocre results in December. The manager of a discount department store in the Tidewater area of Virginia reported little change in recent weeks and noted that 2013 had ended with sales below the previous year. Looking ahead, a representative of central Virginia retailers stated that with Easter falling in late April, merchants have more time for promotions, especially for warm-weather apparel. Retail price growth accelerated moderately.

Services. Revenues at non-retail services firms remained flat since our last report. An executive at a national freight trucking firm reported that he still expects double-digit tonnage growth in the first quarter, despite closed roads and terminals as winter storms moved across the country. However, several other businesses reported no change in demand for their services, and an executive at a wealth management firm in central Virginia described business as "status quo," even with improved client optimism. An executive at a North Carolina healthcare system reported that flu cases were below typical seasonal levels. Services prices edged up at a slightly faster pace.

Tourism was booming at winter resorts, as natural snowfalls were abundant and colder temperatures allowed additional snowmaking. In several locations, mid-February bookings were solid because Valentine's Day and Presidents' Day sandwiched a weekend. However, an hotelier commented that this pushed bookings into one good weekend instead of two. A hotel manager in western North Carolina reported strong bookings and also noted a shift to more transient visits than conference or group bookings in recent weeks. In contrast, a contact in Baltimore saw increased corporate travel. On the Outer Banks of North Carolina, visitors now expect a package "experience" when renting a home, such as included linens, tickets to events, and restaurant coupons.

Finance. Since our last report, consumer borrowing slowed considerably while commercial lending remained strong. Several contacts indicated that residential mortgage lending had nearly come to a halt, in part because of this winter's extreme weather. However, a Virginia lender believed that the demand for new homes is there, but that people are "just trying to survive the weather right now."

Mortgage refinancing activity also declined in most areas. Interest rates flattened recently, after a decline in January. Meanwhile, credit standards remained tight, according to two bankers.

According to sources, commercial lending picked up. Several bankers reported that loan volumes were robust and that they had a healthy pipeline for the future. One lender said that businesses were looking for shorter term commercial real estate loans in order to benefit from the lower interest rates that those loans offer.

Real Estate. Residential real estate strengthened since our last report. Several brokers reported a slight increase in home sales in recent weeks and generally higher sale prices. In addition, buyer traffic and pending sales rose in the past four to six weeks, although a few Realtors noted slowness due to winter weather conditions. A Northern Virginia Realtor commented that sales were more robust than expected, particularly in the high-end market. However, most brokers indicated steady improvement in the $200,000 to $500,000 price range. Realtors reported a mild decrease in housing inventory, with faster absorption in some submarkets.

Construction of multifamily housing remained strong since our last report. In addition, single-family residential construction is returning throughout the district, according to contacts, but has been "slow to come out of the ground" primarily due to weather conditions. Other than in Washington, D.C., non-residential construction was softer. Commercial leasing ranged from unchanged to slightly stronger, with inquiries mainly for small spaces. While most Realtors reported little change in concessions and incentives, some in Washington D.C. and Northern Virginia saw more concessions, in the form of tenant improvements. Reports on vacancy rates varied across location and submarket. Lease rates were unchanged and sale prices rose mildly. Realtors reported either no change or a slight increase in demand for Class A office space.

Agriculture and Natural Resources. According to agriculture contacts, crop prices declined in recent weeks. Falling feed costs and higher cattle prices led contacts to believe it will be a good year for livestock producers. Also, farmers expect an increase in poultry production. However, a North Carolina respondent was concerned about an increase in swine virus in his region. A Virginia nursery owner stated that recent cold weather damage, if any, will not be known for a month or two; even so, he expects a ten percent increase in year-over-year sales this spring. A North Carolina agri-business contact reported that tobacco and vegetable producers in his region were cautiously optimistic for the year ahead. In South Carolina, recent ice storms have caused timber damage that is still being assessed.

Natural gas production remained robust. A West Virginia executive reported "incredible" industry growth and noted that shale gas has fundamentally changed the industry outlook. Contacts remarked that energy prices had risen due to increased demand during the extremely cold weather, and a few businesses reduced usage as a result of the higher cost. An executive also noted that two nuclear power plants are expected to shut down because of high licensing costs. Coal mining continued to soften. Several observers have stated that while steam coal plants experienced closings, metallurgical coal is holding its own—but overall the coal industry is weak at best. In West Virginia, leaking chemicals from a coal processing plant were found in public drinking water, and in North Carolina coal ash was discovered leaking into a river.

Labor Markets. Reports on labor were mixed, as weather-related shutdowns slowed hiring slightly. Demand was strong for semi-skilled workers, project-based laborers, government and healthcare workers, and experienced administrative professionals. Increasingly, quality temporary workers were being offered permanent positions. Turnover remained high among low skill positions. According to our latest survey, retailers reduced employment and average retail wages declined slightly, while non-retail services providers moderately increased payrolls and average wages rose. Manufacturing employment slowed and average wages edged up.

SIXTH DISTRICT – ATLANTA

Sixth District business contacts described economic activity as expanding slowly in January and early February. Some weather related effects were noted for a few sectors late in the period. However, the outlook remains generally optimistic as most contacts expect near-term growth to be sustained at, or slightly above, current levels.

Overall, retailers cited sluggish sales growth for the beginning of the year. The District's tourism industry remained a bright spot with activity being bolstered by international visitors. Homebuilders and brokers noted home sales and prices were above year-ago levels for new and existing homes, while commercial real estate markets continued to witness steady improvements. Manufacturers reported increases in new orders and production. Reports from bankers suggested that loan demand increased for purchases but decreased for refinances. On balance, District employment gains were subdued and prices generally remained stable.

Consumer Spending and Tourism. Merchants reported a slow start to the year with sales growth declining. Many contacts noted that the drop in sales growth was partially attributed to the unusual winter weather experienced in parts of the region. Others indicated that increased healthcare premiums were having a negative impact. Sales for vehicles were lower than expected.

Hospitality contacts reported an increase in business and convention bookings. Reports also indicated that the favorable U.S. dollar exchange rate was a contributing factor to a rise in international visitors. However, contacts did convey that some of the region affected by the unusual winter weather in January and February experienced losses in revenue due to closures of attractions and restaurants, although most hotels were not as adversely affected. Hoteliers still expect only slight growth in occupancy rates for the first quarter of 2014 compared to the same period last year, while room rates and revenue per available room are expected to grow more robustly.

Real Estate and Construction. District brokers indicated that growth in existing home sales had picked up modestly in recent months. Most brokers said sales were slightly up compared with a year earlier and more contacts noted that sales activity was in line with their plan for the period. By most accounts, inventory levels had fallen on a year-over-year basis. The majority of contacts reported that home prices remained ahead of the year earlier level but that price gains have slowed on a month-over-month basis. The outlook among residential brokers continued to improve since our last report.

Reports from District builders were more positive than previous reports. Most contacts agreed that recent activity was in line with their plan for the period. The majority of builders reported that construction activity and new home sales were ahead of the year earlier level, although most reports indicated that unsold inventory levels had remained unchanged from a year ago. The majority of contacts also reported modest home price appreciation. The outlook for new home sales and construction activity remained positive, although many builders expressed concern about dwindling lot inventories and their inability to secure the financing needed to develop new lots.

District brokers noted that demand for commercial real estate continued to improve. Absorption was picking up, although contacts cautioned that the rate of improvement still varied by metropolitan area, submarket, and property type. Construction activity continued to increase at a modest pace from last year; most contacts reported that their backlog was ahead of year earlier levels. Looking ahead, contacts expect that construction activity in apartments will continue to be somewhat strong in 2014 and that there will be a modest increase in construction activity across other property types. The outlook among District commercial real estate contacts remained positive with further improvements expected over the course of the year.

Manufacturing and Transportation. Manufacturing contacts in the region cited expanding activity from January through mid-February, but the pace of growth was moderate. Contacts reported improvements in new orders and production. However, a number of contacts stated that the unusual winter weather affected production in late January and output was lower than planned for that month. That said, nearly two-thirds of purchasing managers polled expect production levels to be higher over the next three to six months.

District transportation firms reported mixed results. Air cargo contacts cited nearly double-digit declines in overall tonnage from a year ago. Port contacts reported year-over-year volume increases in container traffic, bulk cargo, and automotive and machinery. Total rail carloads were down slightly over the same period last year; however, intermodal volumes continued to experience modest gains.

Banking and Finance. Banking and credit union contacts expressed mixed concern about the implementation of the new Qualified Mortgage Rules. Some community bankers reported that they have exited the residential mortgage business altogether because of increased regulatory burdens, while others indicated that they do not believe it will have a negative effect on overall mortgage lending. A number of lenders reported increases in purchase mortgages, but not enough to offset the declines in refinances. Regional credit unions were reportedly offering highly competitive rates on CDs to attract deposits in order to sustain lending activity.

Employment and Prices. Since the last report, job growth remained muted across the District. Contacts in construction, manufacturing, energy, hospitality, and real estate noted modest growth in employment. Trucking companies continued to cite driver shortages even amidst rising pay. Rather than adding to payrolls, businesses reportedly continued to rely on technology to enhance output. Some employers continued to show reluctance in large-scale hiring due to concerns about healthcare reform.

Most contacts reported modest and relatively stable labor and material cost pressures. Construction industry contacts remained a notable exception, indicating strong upward pressure on labor costs and some materials prices. According to the Atlanta Fed's February business inflation expectations (BIE) survey, costs were up 1.7 percent from a year ago and were expected to pick up slightly to 2.0 percent over the coming 12 months. In general, businesses continued to indicate that they had little to no pricing power.

Natural Resources and Agriculture. Strong production growth coupled with higher pipeline capacity continued to supply Gulf Coast refiners with ample light sweet crude. Natural gas storage levels were reported as notably low due to increased withdrawals that were exacerbated by the unusually severe weather. Commercial and residential demand for utilities increased significantly as a result of the weather, yet industrial usage remained fairly consistent with seasonal norms. The energy industry remains optimistic regarding their outlook for demand, pricing, and productivity.

Recent rains improved soil conditions in parts of Florida and Georgia while portions of Alabama, Louisiana, Mississippi, and Tennessee experienced dry soil conditions. Meanwhile, freezing temperatures and cold winds had farmers and livestock producers taking precautions to mitigate damage to crops and livestock throughout much of the District. There were mixed reports of the impact on Florida crops with some indicating damage to vegetable and strawberry crops and others suggesting no damage to citrus. However, the Florida citrus crop continues to be adversely affected by citrus greening causing diminished production and increased expense battling the disease. On a year-over-year basis, prices paid to farmers for corn, soybeans, hogs, and broilers were down; while cotton, rice, oranges, beef, and eggs were up. The most recent domestic crop production forecasts for corn, rice, soybeans, oranges, and cotton were unchanged from a month ago. Similarly, pork and broilers projections were down moderately while beef projections were up slightly.

SEVENTH DISTRICT—CHICAGO

Summary. Growth in economic activity in the Seventh District slowed in January and February, as severe winter weather affected activity in a number of sectors. The modest pace of growth to start the year tempered contacts' expectations only somewhat, as most generally maintained their optimistic outlook for 2014. Growth in consumer and business spending slowed. Manufacturing production growth and construction activity were modest. Credit conditions were little changed on balance. Cost pressures remained generally mild, though extreme temperatures caused energy prices to spike. Prices for corn, soybeans, and livestock were up slightly.

Consumer spending. Growth in consumer spending slowed to a modest pace in January and February. Some retail categories initially benefitted from the poor winter weather, in large part reflecting increased outlays for necessities. However, retail contacts said that once necessary items were purchased, the persistent bad weather led to declining customer traffic and sales. Auto dealers also noted that the weather contributed to lower showroom traffic and sales. However, some contacts pointed to wavering consumer confidence as an alternative reason for lower auto sales. Many dealers expected incentives to increase in the near-term in an effort to rejuvenate sales.

Business spending. Growth in business spending also slowed to a modest pace in January and February. Inventories remained at comfortable levels for most retailers and manufacturers. Growth in capital spending slowed somewhat, while plans for future capital expenditures edged higher. Several manufacturing contacts reported plans to purchase new equipment to increase capacity. Contacts in the manufacturing, banking and finance, and retail sectors reported plans for expansion, either by building or buying new structures or through mergers and acquisitions. The pace of hiring slowed, as did expectations of future hiring, though expectations for the coming year remained positive. A staffing firm reported continued growth in demand for its industrial services, despite some weather-related closures. In contrast, growth in demand for its professional services weakened. A banking contact noted an increase in layoffs due to declining mortgage refinancing. Many contacts noted continuing strength in the demand for skilled workers, with positions often difficult to fill in engineering, information technology, accounting, and other technical occupations.

Construction and real estate. Construction and real estate activity again increased modestly in January and February. However, the pace of growth slowed over the reporting period, with homebuilders reporting that the unusually cold weather had added to costs and led to construction delays. The weather also affected home sales, as several contacts indicated that the cold had dampened new buyer activity. Overall, however, the housing market continued to improve slowly, with home prices and residential rents rising modestly. Real estate brokers noted that the supply of homes for sale remains low, and many homes continue to be purchased with cash because lending standards remain tight. In addition, several contacts indicated that the continued limited availability of new construction financing has kept new home inventories near record lows. Nonresidential construction grew slowly, with one contact noting that industrial building activity had paused in recent weeks. Commercial real estate activity ticked up, as vacancies declined and rents rose. Niche, high-income properties remain a source of strength for the sector, particularly for restaurants and office buildings.

Manufacturing. Manufacturing production growth slowed to a modest pace in January and February, as unusually bad winter weather dampened the demand for manufactured goods and disrupted supply chains. However, manufacturing contacts remained optimistic, generally believing that overall economic conditions remained positive. The auto industry remained a source of strength for the District, even with a weather-related slowdown in sales. The weather also had a significant effect on the demand for steel, though contacts were preparing to meet any pent-up demand that developed during the reporting period. The severe weather conditions also affected the production and transportation of goods. For example, a steel industry contact reported that there were seven days in the last six weeks where his firm could not send shipments, a first in his thirty-five years of experience. Steel service centers reported reduced demand, while specialty metal manufacturers cited mixed but overall modest growth in new orders. Manufacturers of construction materials noted fewer shipments because of the weather, but continued to have a positive near-term outlook for the housing market. Demand for heavy machinery remained soft, as weakness in the mining and agricultural industries overshadowed increasing strength in the construction and energy industries.

Banking/finance. Credit conditions were little changed on balance over the reporting period. Equity market volatility increased and corporate bond spreads widened some. Banking contacts reported slow but steady growth in business loan demand, but greater demand for purchases of equipment and owner-occupied real estate. Activity in the leveraged loan market picked up, with contacts noting increased competition from commercial finance companies and greater demand on the secondary market. Agricultural contacts reported that banks were helping farms restructure costs for the coming season to shore up margins. However, in some cases troubled farmers were forced to search for new lenders when denied credit. Growth in consumer loan demand remained modest, again led by the relative strength of auto lending. Contacts noted moderate downward pressure on pricing and standards across a variety of loan categories.

Prices/costs. Cost pressures remained mild overall. However, the severe winter weather pushed up prices for energy commodities, creating supply shortages and disruptive price spikes in some areas, especially for propane and natural gas. For instance, a contact reported that a grain elevator withdrew its propane from storage and resold it for home use. Another business contact reported that because homes have priority in natural gas delivery, her company faced a supply shortage and was forced to shift its production schedule. Other producers chose to delay production rather than pay high prices. Most contacts expected energy markets to return to normal once warmer weather arrives. Prices for cement, drywall, lumber, copper, and rare earth metals rose. Prices for steel, scrap, and iron ore were lower even though the winter weather interrupted shipments. Wage pressures edged up, and were stronger for skilled workers. Many contacts indicated that non-wage labor costs increased because of higher healthcare premiums.

Agriculture. Severe winter weather disrupted the flow of agricultural products between farms and markets during the reporting period. Crops that were sold stayed on farms longer than intended as transportation problems delayed shipments. Contacts also reported shortages of trucks and drivers to deliver inventories from the large harvest last fall. Demand for crops has been better than expected, particularly for corn, pushing inventories lower and prices higher. Soybean prices drifted up as uncertainty regarding the harvest in South America weighed on markets. Concerns about high costs for land rentals were also widespread. Livestock producers reported improving bottom lines driven by higher prices for milk, hogs, and cattle combined with lower feed costs. However, some hog farms reported losses of young pigs because of disease. Dairy producers have seen a boost in demand from exports.

Eighth District - St. Louis

Summary

The economy of the Eighth District has continued to grow at a moderate pace since the previous survey. Recent reports of planned activity in manufacturing have been positive, while reports in services have been negative on net. Residential and commercial real estate market conditions have continued to improve. Lending at a sample of District banks was little changed during the fourth quarter of 2013. Wage increases have been moderate, while prices and employment levels have increased modestly.

Consumer Spending

Contacts reported that retail sales in the past three months increased slightly compared with the same period last year. Two thirds of contacts noted somewhat higher sales, while one third saw no change. Half of the retailers reported that sales levels met their expectations, while the other half reported that sales were below expectations. Three fourths of contacts noted that inventories were at desired levels, and the rest noted that inventories were too low. Three fourths of contacts noted no change in the mix of high- and low-end products, while the rest noted more sales of high-end relative to low-end products.

Reports from auto dealers about sales in the past three months were mixed. One in four car dealers surveyed saw increased sales compared with the same period last year; half saw no change, and the rest saw decreased sales. Half of contacts reported an increase in used car sales relative to new car sales; 12 percent reported the opposite, and the rest saw no change. Thirty-eight percent of contacts reported increased sales of low-end vehicles relative to high-end vehicles; 25 percent reported the opposite, and the rest saw no change. Sixty-three percent of contacts noted that inventories were at desired levels, while 37 percent noted that inventories were too high.

Manufacturing and Other Business Activity

Reports of plans for manufacturing activity have been positive since our previous report. Several manufacturing firms reported plans to add workers or expand operations in the Eighth District, while a smaller number of manufacturers reported plans to reduce employment. Firms in automobile, plastic products, auto parts, appliance, food, alcoholic beverage, and machinery manufacturing plan to hire new employees and expand operations in the Eighth District. In contrast, firms that manufacture television sets, semiconductor devices, metal products, and carbonated beverages reported plans to lay off workers. According to a recent survey, manufacturers saw increased sales over the past three months, compared with a year ago. Several industrial contacts noted disruptions in operations because of cold weather; disruptions included gas or electricity outages, difficulty commuting to work, and delays in logistics.

Reports of planned activity in the District's service sector have been negative on net since the previous report. Firms in mortgage, telephone answering, disinfecting and pest control, pharmaceutical benefit management, and social security benefit management services reported plans to lay off workers or reduce employee hours. In contrast, firms in health care, telecommunication, computer-system consulting, legal, fitness and recreation, online shopping, and food distribution services reported new hiring and expansion plans in the District.

Real Estate and Construction

Home sales have continued to increase throughout most of the Eighth District on a year-over-year basis. Compared with the same period in 2012, December 2013 year-to-date home sales were up 16 percent in Louisville, 17 percent in Little Rock, 7 percent in Memphis, and 4 percent in St. Louis. December 2013 year-to-date single-family housing permits increased in the largest metro areas of the District, compared with the same period in 2012. Permits increased 8 percent in Louisville, 12 percent in Memphis, and 11 percent in St. Louis. In contrast, permits decreased 9 percent in Little Rock.

Commercial and industrial real estate market conditions in the District have continued to improve. A contact in northwest Kentucky reported that office leasing continued to struggle while the demand for industrial space continued to improve. A contact in northeast Arkansas noted modest improvement in commercial real estate. A contact in northwest St. Louis County reported that office leasing in 2013 increased for the fourth consecutive year and expected a strong start in 2014. Commercial and industrial construction improved throughout most of the District. A contact in Louisville noted several on-going commercial construction projects in Hardin County, Kentucky, and in downtown Louisville. Contacts in Memphis continued to report new commercial construction in Jonesboro and

Paragould. A contact noted a new office building project in northwest St. Louis County and a new industrial manufacturing plant in Wentzville, Missouri. A contact in Little Rock reported a plan for a mixed-use project that includes commercial space and a plan for an outlet mall in Little Rock.

Banking and Finance

A survey of District banks found little change in overall lending activity during the fourth quarter of 2013. During this period, credit standards and creditworthiness of applicants for commercial and industrial loans increased slightly, while demand improved moderately and delinquencies decreased moderately. Credit standards and creditworthiness of applicants for prime residential mortgage loans increased moderately. Demand was much weaker overall, with some respondents reporting substantial weakness, and delinquencies decreased moderately. Credit standards and creditworthiness for auto loans and credit cards remained mostly unchanged, while demand decreased moderately and delinquencies edged down slightly. Credit standards, creditworthiness of applicants, demand, and delinquencies for other consumer loans decreased.

Agriculture and Natural Resources

Red meat production in the District for 2013 was 1.2 percent higher than in 2012. The production increase was driven by the District's largest producers in Illinois, Indiana, and Missouri. Coal production in the District for January 2014 was 6.2 percent lower compared with January 2013.

Prices, Wages, and Employment

A survey of Eighth District businesses indicated that wages grew at a moderate pace, while prices and employment increased modestly over the past three months. Sixty-seven percent of contacts reported that prices during the past three months remained about the same relative to the same period last year, while 21 percent of contacts indicated that prices were somewhat higher. Fifty-seven percent of respondents indicated that wages during the past three months have stayed about the same relative to a year ago, while 33 percent noted somewhat higher wages. Finally, 72 percent of contacts reported that employment levels have remained the same over the past three months, compared with a year ago, while 20 percent reported an increase and 11 percent reported a decrease.

NINTH DISTRICT--MINNEAPOLIS

The Ninth District economy experienced moderate growth since the last report. Increased activity was noted in consumer spending, residential and commercial construction, commercial real estate, professional services, manufacturing, and energy and mining. Tourism was mixed, while residential real estate activity decreased and agricultural conditions weakened for farmers. Labor markets tightened since the last report, and wage increases were moderate. Prices generally remained level with a few exceptions noted.

Consumer Spending and Tourism

Retail sales activity increased moderately. A Minnesota-based restaurant and bar chain reported that recent same-store sales were up 2 percent to 5 percent from a year ago. A mall manager in Minnesota noted that apparel retailers reported an increase in resort wear sales and that restaurants and bars were busy. Two furniture retailers were expanding showroom space in North Dakota and Montana. A car dealership in Minnesota noted that mechanics were working overtime to meet demand for repairs in large part due to cold, wintry weather. A Montana auto dealer reported solid sales activity in January.

Tourism was mixed, as extremely cold weather was balanced by strong snow depth in several areas of the district. Cold weather slowed the number of visitors to the Upper Peninsula of Michigan. A Minnesota ski resort reported that cold weather slowed ski lift sales on a number of days. However, several ski resorts in Montana reported that lift ticket sales and lodging were up over last year, as the region benefited from good snow conditions. Looking ahead, Minneapolis' convention and tourism bureau anticipates that attendance at events in 2014 will be the largest in more than 10 years.

Construction and Real Estate

Commercial construction activity continued to grow since the last report. New hotels are planned or under construction in several Minnesota markets. In the Minneapolis-St. Paul area, a large retail mall and several industrial as well as mixed-use developments were planned. The retail vacancy rate dropped 50 basis points in the fourth quarter from the third quarter of 2013 in the Minneapolis-St. Paul area. However, the value of January commercial permits in Sioux Falls, S.D., was down slightly from a year ago. Overall residential construction activity increased. In the Minneapolis-St. Paul area, the value of January residential permits grew by 28 percent from January 2013. The value of January multifamily residential building permits in Billings, Mont., increased from January 2013, but single-family decreased. The value of January residential building permits in Sioux Falls decreased significantly from a year earlier.

Activity in commercial real estate markets increased since the last report. A recent report by a Minneapolis-St. Paul area real estate analytics firm noted that absorption of space is solid and that investors expect more activity across all property types. Residential real estate market activity decreased since the last report. In the Sioux Falls area, January home sales were down 13 percent and inventory was down 4 percent, while the median sale price increased 5 percent relative to a year earlier. In La Crosse, Wis., January home sales and the median price decreased from January 2013. Meanwhile, January home sales were down 13 percent from the same period a year ago in the Minneapolis area; the inventory of homes for sale was down 11 percent, while the median sale price rose 12 percent.

Services

Activity at professional business services firms increased since the last report. A February Minneapolis Fed ad hoc survey of lawyers, accountants, engineers, architects, IT consultants and other professional business services firms noted optimism. Most respondents expected more orders and increasing billable hours. A lawyer noted that transactional activity was up and that clients' business increased during the past two years; the lawyer expected this to continue. Recent revenue was up at several Minnesota advertising agencies compared with a year earlier.

Manufacturing

District manufacturing activity increased moderately since the last report. Purchasing managers responding to a January survey by Creighton University (Omaha, Neb.) reported that manufacturing activity increased in Minnesota and the Dakotas. A company in the early stages of planning a $1.7 billion nitrogen fertilizer plant in North Dakota exceeded its fundraising goals. South Dakota's state government withdrew $13 million in loan commitments for a shuttered Aberdeen beef slaughter plant that declared bankruptcy and was sold last December.

Energy and Mining

Activity in the energy sector remained brisk. Mid-February oil and gas exploration in Montana and North Dakota decreased slightly from recent months, primarily due to extreme cold; however, production remains at record levels. Unexpected demand for propane to dry corn at harvest time, along with severe cold, led to a surge in demand for the fuel. A judge's decision opened the doors for approval of a $250 million solar power development in Minnesota. Overall mining activity was stable. District iron ore mines were operating at near capacity. Meanwhile, fourth quarter 2013 palladium and platinum production was up in Montana compared with the same period in 2012.

Agriculture

Conditions continued to soften for district farmers, while livestock and dairy producers remained in better shape. More than half of respondents to the Minneapolis Fed's fourth quarter (January) Survey of Agricultural Credit Conditions said farm incomes decreased in the last three months of 2013, and two-thirds expected incomes to fall in the first quarter of this year. Cattle and hog producers continued to benefit from high prices and falling feed costs, as did dairy producers, according to survey comments. Informal survey results suggest that farmers are reacting to falling corn prices and intend to plant fewer acres of corn and a potentially record high acreage of soybeans this coming spring. January prices received by farmers fell from a year earlier for corn, wheat, soybeans, hogs and chickens; prices increased for cattle, milk, eggs and turkeys.

Employment, Wages and Prices

Labor markets tightened slightly since the last report. A software company expansion in North Dakota will result in 150 construction jobs, followed by increased employment of up to 180 new workers over the next few years. A home improvement retailer announced plans to hire about 1,000 workers in the Minneapolis-St. Paul area to fill spring positions. A workforce center in western Minnesota noted strong demand for welders and health care workers, such as certified nursing assistants. In contrast, a Minnesota-based retailer announced plans to lay off 400 to 500 employees, while another Minnesota company will lay off more than 180 employees in its legal publishing division. A printing plant in Minnesota will close, laying off 170 workers.

Overall wage increases were moderate. Wages remained at high levels in the oil-drilling areas of North Dakota and Montana, but the pace of increase has moderated recently.

Prices were generally level with a few exceptions noted. Minnesota gasoline prices remained level since the last report. Some metals prices were down slightly. Meanwhile, District consumers of residential propane faced prices two to three times higher than a year ago due to strong demand and supply constraints.

TENTH DISTRICT – KANSAS CITY

The Tenth District economy remained stable in January and February and was expected to improve during the next few months. Consumer spending declined moderately as a decrease in automobile, retail, and restaurant sales outweighed an increase in tourism activity. Manufacturing activity expanded moderately, and expectations for future activity remained positive. Construction and residential real estate activity decreased slightly, while commercial real estate activity strengthened. Contacts anticipated stronger real estate and construction activity in the coming months as the weather improves and demand remains strong. Bankers continued to report steady overall loan demand, improved loan quality, and stable deposit levels. Agricultural growing conditions for winter wheat deteriorated, while livestock and crop prices edged higher. Energy activity remained strong, and capital expenditures were expected to increase along with drilling activity. Prices increased slightly for both finished goods and raw materials, with further gains expected in the next few months. Wages rose modestly in most industries, and contacts continued to report difficulty finding workers for some skilled positions.

Consumer Spending. Consumer spending declined moderately in January and February but was expected to increase modestly in the coming months. Contacts noted a variety of reasons for the recent slowdown including typical seasonal patterns, extreme winter weather, regulatory and political uncertainty, and a softening in consumer confidence. Although retail sales fell over the past month, sales remained slightly above year-ago levels. Automobile sales decreased moderately in recent months and fell to levels that were well below one year ago. However, automobile inventories continued to build, and contacts anticipated modest improvement in sales over the next few months. Restaurant sales also dipped sharply in February, but were consistent with year-ago levels and were expected to rise in the next few months. Tourism activity was significantly stronger than one year ago, with hotel occupancy rates and room rates both higher. Increased snowfall improved skiing conditions in the District and led to more ski-related tourism.

Manufacturing and Other Business Activity. Manufacturing and transportation activity increased moderately since the last survey period, while other business activity was unchanged. Manufacturing activity picked up for both durable goods and nondurable goods, with production, shipments and new orders expanding at a faster pace among durable goods manufacturers. Overall, manufacturing activity and capital expenditures remained above year-ago levels, and expectations for the future were positive. Contacts in professional and high-tech services, healthcare services, and wholesale trade reported roughly stable sales since the last survey period and anticipated activity to pick up in the coming months. Transportation companies reported stronger sales in February, and contacts were increasingly optimistic about future activity.

Real Estate and Construction. Construction and residential real estate sales decreased slightly, while commercial real estate activity strengthened from the previous survey period. Residential sales declined slightly, while inventories remained low and fell further. Low- and medium-priced homes continued to drive sales, while higher-priced home sales remained sluggish in most of the District. Residential realtors reported additional home price gains, and expected residential real estate activity to improve in the near-term as demand increases due to seasonality. Builders reported that the number of starts was flat during the survey period, but construction activity was expected to strengthen in the coming months, with prices and buyer traffic both expected to increase. Mortgage activity fell slightly compared to the last survey period and compared to a year ago, but was expected to increase in the coming months as a rise in home purchase loans was anticipated to outweigh the decrease in refinancings. Commercial real estate contacts reported a decline in vacancy rates, a slight increase in absorption, and higher sales. Commercial real estate construction softened slightly but was still up over last year and was expected to increase in the coming months.

Banking. Bankers reported steady overall loan demand, improved loan quality, and stable deposit levels in February. Most respondents reported steady demand for commercial and industrial loans, commercial real estate loans, consumer installment loans, and agriculture loans. Demand for residential real estate loans declined during the survey period. Bankers reported improved loan quality compared to a year ago, and all bankers expected the outlook for loan quality to either improve or remain the same over the next six months. Credit standards remained unchanged in all major loan categories, and respondents reported stable deposits.

Agriculture. Crop growing conditions deteriorated, while livestock prices strengthened since the last survey period. Slightly more than half of the winter wheat crop was rated in fair to poor condition as scattered snowfalls provided only marginal soil moisture. Crop prices edged up from recent lows due to an uptick in export demand and concern that South American corn and soybean production would be lower than previously expected. Feeder cattle prices rose further with historically low cow inventories, and strong export demand supported higher fed cattle prices. Hog prices rose amid an intensifying swine virus outbreak that was expected to constrain pork supplies. In addition, production costs for livestock feeders edged down due to lower feed prices. Agricultural bankers indicated that farmland price appreciation moderated from the rapid pace seen the past few years, and most expected values would level off in 2014.

Energy. District energy activity remained solid in January and February and was expected to remain steady in the coming months. Oil rigs increased slightly in the District, particularly in Oklahoma and Colorado. Natural gas rigs edged down despite the surge in natural gas spot prices and record-high withdrawals from storage. Although futures prices for March and April natural gas contracts have risen recently, energy contacts expected natural gas prices to decrease slightly in the coming weeks as storage is restocked. Crude oil prices were expected to remain steady. Propane prices increased significantly for many consumers due to already low propane stocks and unusually cold weather. Capital expenditures were projected to increase in the coming months, particularly in drilling for oil and natural gas liquids.

Wages and Prices. Prices of finished goods increased modestly, while raw material prices rose moderately in January and February. Wages ticked up and were expected to continue to move higher in the months ahead. Retail, automobile, restaurant and manufacturing contacts noted price increases for both inputs and finished products. However, raw material prices were reportedly rising at a faster pace. These contacts anticipated additional price increases in the months ahead. Builders also reported an uptick in the price of construction materials, particularly roofing. Wages rose modestly in most industries, with transportation and automobile contacts reporting larger increases. Retail and restaurant respondents expected wages to increase at a faster pace over the next six months after minimal gains in recent months. Contacts in the professional and technical services, construction, and transportation industries expected the largest wage gains in the coming months. Some contacts continued to report difficulty finding skilled workers including technicians, engineers, construction trade laborers, and experienced supervisors.

ELEVENTH DISTRICT—DALLAS

Summary   The Eleventh District Economy grew at a moderate pace over the past six weeks. Manufacturing activity increased overall, although there were a few reports of slowing demand. Retail and automobile sales were slightly weaker but contacts' outlooks were positive. Demand improved in most nonfinancial services industries with the exception of transportation services, which was negatively impacted by severe national weather. Sales of new single-family homes remained on an upward trend, and office and industrial real estate leasing activity remained strong. Loan demand held relatively steady. Energy activity remained solid, while agricultural conditions worsened. Price increases were noted in several industries, although most were modest. Outlooks were optimistic across most industries.

Prices   Most responding firms said prices were stable to up slightly over the reporting period. There were a few instances of accelerating prices. Fabricated metals producers noted continued increases in selling prices and expect more in the next six months. Food producers said that selling prices had moved up due to rising input costs, especially for dairy and beef. One airline reported a modest increase in ticket prices. Some transportation firms expected increases in shipping rates in coming months due to higher fuel costs. Retail prices were stable overall and auto selling prices were unchanged.

Natural gas prices rose marginally over the course of the last six weeks, peaking at $7.63 in early February and ending the reporting period at $5.35. This was driven by the exceptionally cold winter, which led to a drawdown of inventories to the bottom of its 5-year range. The price of WTI also rose over the last six weeks, trading as high as $100.35 at the end of the period. This price behavior was driven in part by heating oil demand, which has also been bolstered by the severe winter, and debottlenecking at Cushing, OK.

Labor Market   Employment levels held steady or increased slightly at most responding firms. Staffing firms said employment levels were up modestly and expected to hire additional workers. Accounting and legal firms reported a modest increase in employment levels. One transportation services firm expected to increase payrolls significantly this year while another one continued with an incentivized buyout to reduce employment. Fabricated metals and food manufacturing firms reported increased hiring due to stronger demand. A recreational vehicle producer noted employment was up moderately and expected to continue hiring. Labor shortages were reported for engineers, truck drivers, mechanics, machinists and construction workers.

There were some reports of upward wage pressure. High-tech respondents noted moderate wage pressure for high-skilled workers including electrical engineers. Primary metals contacts and food producers noted slight increases in wage pressures for skilled and technical workers. Airlines reported upward pressure on wages, and one airline had increased salaries modestly. In addition, a transportation services firm noted wages were up slightly, and accounting contacts reported marginal wage pressure. Single-family housing contacts continued to note rising wage pressures.

Manufacturing Reports from manufacturers were mostly positive and outlooks were optimistic. Construction–related manufacturers said that demand increased since the last report, despite bad weather locally. Fabricated metals producers reported strong demand, a result of robust commercial and residential construction. Contacts noted demand is well above last year's levels. Demand for primary metals softened seasonally since the last report, although most contacts said demand was somewhat better than this time last year. Energy-related manufacturing contacts and food producers noted steady demand at healthy levels. Paper manufacturers said demand was flat to up and running slightly ahead of expectations. Demand for transportation equipment was mixed, in part due to bad weather in the region, but it was still well above year-ago levels.

Contacts in high-tech manufacturing reported a slight improvement in orders since the last survey period. Responding firms said that demand for memory chips remained strong and demand for logic devices remained weak but stable. Inventories were reported as stable and employment levels were flat to slightly up. Most contacts expect stronger demand this year as they expect the world economy to pick up moderately and replacement rates of high tech devices to increase.

Refinery contacts noted that utilization rates fell slightly, in part due to weather effects. The production growth of major chemicals was mixed. Refinery and petrochemical margins remained healthy.

Retail Sales Retail sales were a little weaker this reporting period due in part to bad weather nationally but year-over-year growth remained positive. According to three national retailers, demand in Texas slightly outperformed the nation since the last report. Contacts' outlooks for the rest of this quarter and the remainder of the year are positive.

Automobile sales softened slightly since the previous report. In north Texas, this was attributed to cold weather. Year-over-year demand ranged from down slightly to up slightly. Inventory levels varied by manufacturer, and generally were not a source of concern. Contacts' outlooks for the remainder of the quarter and the year were mostly optimistic.

Nonfinancial Services Staffing firms said demand was up more than expected, and that they plan to increase hiring. One contact noted requests for IT professionals started rising again after maintaining an already high level over the past several months. Contacts were more optimistic than at the time of the last report. Accounting firms said demand continued to trend upward, although there was some softness in tax services. Outlooks were cautiously positive. Legal firms noted a slight increase in demand over the past six weeks and it was up notably from last year. Transportation service firms noted mixed demand. Railroad cargo volumes fell slightly below year-ago levels, with severe weather nationally largely to blame. Coal, grain and nonmetallic minerals saw good growth, and chemicals and petroleum shipments rose modestly. Weakness was seen in shipments of lumber and wood and motor vehicles. The outlook remained positive with strong growth expected in the first part of 2014. Small parcel shipping decelerated since the last report but was up from a year ago. Retail trade continued to be the largest driver of growth, and the outlook was optimistic. Air cargo volumes were up since the last report but down slightly from a year ago. Respondents in the maritime shipping industry said loaded container volume declined slightly, but that for 2013 as a whole container volumes rose moderately.

Airline demand was solid to slightly stronger according to contacts. Severe winter weather across the nation caused some temporary disruptions, but demand rebounded quickly. Demand was in line with or slightly above year ago levels. Outlooks were optimistic.

Construction and Real Estate   Single-family home sales remained on an upward trend over the past six weeks, although one contact noted a slight slowdown in the pace of new home sales in recent weeks. Inventories of new and existing homes remained at extremely low levels. One respondent noted the low inventory of developed lots could hamper single-family building activity later in the year. Apartment demand remained solid and construction activity continued at high levels. Rental rate growth was above the historical average in most major metros. One contact was concerned about possible overbuilding in urban areas.

Office and industrial leasing activity was strong. Sales activity remained at high levels and contacts expect it to increase this year, noting a more friendly lending environment. Outlooks were positive and commercial development is expected to continue to rise this year.

Financial Services   Financial sector performance remained relatively level over the past six weeks. Demand improved marginally for commercial real estate, middle-market, mergers and acquisitions, and consumer loans. Some softness was reported in residential real estate lending. Loan pricing remained relatively unchanged at competitive levels, and loan quality continued to strengthen. Deposit volumes increased slightly on net after fluctuations in the beginning of the year; rates remain low and static. Respondents' outlooks are hopeful for a better year, noting less client uncertainty and potentially growing interest in loans.

Energy   Eleventh District demand for oil field services remained healthy over the past six weeks. Contacts noted that activity in Texas is particularly strong, both inland and offshore, and they were moderately more optimistic for the first half of 2014 than in prior reporting periods.

Agriculture   After gradually easing throughout the fall, district drought conditions worsened slightly in January and early February. Wheat crop and pasture conditions deteriorated somewhat due to lack of sufficient rainfall. Cotton prices have rallied since December, which may lead more farmers to favor cotton over other row crops when making planting decisions this spring.

TWELFTH DISTRICT–SAN FRANCISCO

Summary

Economic activity in the Twelfth District expanded at a moderate pace during the reporting period of late December through mid-February. Price increases for most final goods and services were minimal, and wage gains remained quite modest on net. The pace of retail sales stepped down, although demand for business and consumer services rose. District manufacturing activity was mixed. Production activity in agricultural and resource-related industries expanded on balance. Activity in residential and commercial real estate markets continued to expand. Financial institutions reported that loan demand increased overall.

Prices and Wages

Contacts observed minimal price increases for most final goods and services. Fruit and produce prices moved up, and many contacts expect food and water price inflation to pick up in the near term as a consequence of the drought in California. Prices edged up for some construction-related inputs, including wood, insulation, and cement. A higher supply of recycled metals in Asia resulted in lower exports of such metals from the United States, which contributed to downward pressure on U.S. steel input costs and on final prices for steel products.

Wage gains remained quite modest on net, although contacts pointed to signs of building upward wage pressures in areas with particularly strong regional economic activity. Wages for some worker types, notably software developers and engineers, continued to increase rapidly. Reports suggested that the rising cost of living in the San Francisco Bay Area may be pushing up wage pressures.

Retail Trade and Services

The pace of retail sales stepped down. Traditional brick-and-mortar retailers faced fierce competition from online vendors, but recent reports indicated that both in-store and online sales were soft. Retail grocers observed increasing price sensitivity on the part of consumers and noted that even upscale retail grocery establishments experienced pressure on margins. Despite the recognition of some weakness in current conditions, most contacts expect consumer spending to improve or stay the same over the next

12 months. In particular, contacts were optimistic in their outlook for spending on autos and home furnishings.

Demand for business and consumer services rose. Demand for cloud computing services remained strong, although contacts noted that many small and medium-sized businesses have continued to invest in their own data centers. Contacts noted that activity in the food service industry continued to improve. Providers of health-care services expect increased demand for services as a result of expanded coverage under the Affordable Care Act. The level of Hawaiian travel and tourism activity in 2013 surpassed past-year records despite a slowdown in the fourth quarter. Contacts also indicated that tourism picked up in Southern California, with occupancy rates in San Diego hotels reaching historic highs. Overall tourism conditions in Las Vegas improved slightly.

Manufacturing

District manufacturing activity was mixed during the reporting period of late December through mid-February. Contacts noted that year-over-year growth in the electronic components industry resumed after several quarters of decline. Semiconductor sales hit record levels in 2013 and are expected to grow modestly in 2014. The sustained backlog of orders for commercial aircraft supported growth in the commercial aerospace industry, although contacts expect the pace of new orders to slow this year. Defense-related manufacturers reported sluggish overall conditions, and they expect sales, new orders, and capacity utilization to trend downward. Wood and steel product manufacturers noted that extreme weather conditions across the country created problems along their supply chains. Demand for steel used in private nonresidential construction projects continued to improve slowly, although contacts reported low capacity utilization rates at steel mills.

Agriculture and Resource-related Industries

Production in agricultural and resource-related industries expanded on balance. Demand was stable for most crop and livestock products. Concerns about water costs and availability may cause farmers in the California Central Valley to scale back planting. Contacts expect growers to allocate water to more permanent plantings, such as almond and walnut orchards, before allocating water to annual crops, such as corn. In addition, dairy and meat producers may face higher feed costs due to water shortages. Year-over-year crude oil production increased robustly, although consumer demand for petroleum and gasoline rose more modestly. Demand for electricity and gas by industrial customers grew further.

Real Estate and Construction

Activity in residential and commercial real estate markets continued to expand. Home prices across most of the District climbed further, albeit at a bit slower pace, and contacts indicated that the pace of home sales was below historical averages in many areas. Contacts noted that while mortgage application volume in Idaho increased, completed sales transactions dropped. Most contacts expect homebuilding activity to strengthen this year. Occupancy rates for commercial real estate trended up in some areas, and increasing permit activity and sales of empty lots suggest that commercial construction may pick up further. In other areas, contacts noted that existing available square footage, especially in retail-oriented properties, has stifled new construction. Public infrastructure projects, as well as a large number of high-rise commercial construction projects, have been announced or are under way in Honolulu, Seattle, Los Angeles, and the San Francisco Bay Area.

Financial Institutions

Financial institutions reported that loan demand increased overall. Lending grew robustly in selected areas, and contacts noted that asset quality improved at most banks. Contacts noted that credit remains cheap and available for large firms but less accessible by smaller businesses. Ample liquidity in the marketplace continued to perpetuate substantial competition among lenders for business from high-quality commercial borrowers. Contacts indicated that some financial institutions relaxed underwriting standards in an effort to win new business or maintain existing business relationships. In the District's Internet and digital media sectors, there were several notable mergers and acquisitions during the reporting period, and the pace of initial public offerings picked up slightly. Private equity activity was mostly stable, and venture capital financing was strong. The volume of venture capital deals in the second half of 2013 reached mid-2007 levels, and the value of deals surged in the fourth quarter of 2013.